Radio Times

BRAINBOX

P·U·Z·Z·L·E B·O·O·K

2

Radio Times

BRAINBOX

P·U·Z·Z·L·E B·O·O·K

2

BY
CLIVE DOIG

BBC BOOKS

Acknowledgements

The author wishes to thank the following for all the help they have given in the preparation of this book:

Nick Brett, John Collis, Julia and Natasha Doig, Julian Flanders, Sarah Amit, and most especially Marianna Shackcloth.

Published by BBC Books,
a division of BBC Enterprises Limited,
Woodlands, 80 Wood Lane, London W12 0TT

First Published 1990

© Clive Doig 1990

ISBN 0 563 36116 6

Set in Plantin by Ace Filmsetting Ltd
Printed and bound in Britain by Martins of Berwick Ltd
Cover printed by Clays Ltd, St Ives plc

CONTENTS

INTRODUCTION

This second book of my Brainbox Puzzles again includes some mindbending logic, mathematical and word association conundrums, which have appeared in the pages of the *Radio Times* over the last few years. I have also included a number of the ever-popular TRACKWORDS for readers to solve.

To set the record straight I must just answer a couple of the many questions that I am always being asked:

Yes, I do work out all the possible words that can be tracked through the TRACKWORD grid. I use a wonderful book called *Chambers Words*, that lists all the main entry words in the *Chambers Twentieth Century Dictionary* (now called the *Chambers English Dictionary*).

The list of words that I finally arrive at, unfortunately, often includes obscure and obsolete words, words of vulgar or coloquial usage, and most especially Scottish words. These words are often way beyond my knowledge of vocabulary, but I do include most of them in my 'total words' lists printed at the back of the book. My 'average' and 'brainbox' figures are slightly arbitrary in that the latter figure is based on the words I recognise, and the 'average' figure is based on the words I would expect the average reader to know. I apologise that on occasion I do miss some words that can be legitimately tracked through the grid.

The rules for acceptable words state that no foreign words or proper nouns are allowed, and no plurals which require the addition of a single 's' are allowed either. However, other derivatives of basic root words are allowed (for instance the addition of -er or -ed).

Yes! I do think up, devise, compile and write all the puzzles that appear in the *Radio Times* and that are reproduced in this book. They are therefore original puzzles and naturally the solutions to them are likewise original. This does mean, I will be honest, that until they appear in the *Radio Times*, no one has set their mind to solving them, other than myself. However, a number of times, readers far more clever than I, do come up with better, more accurate, alternative or sometimes the correct answer, where I have got it wrong. I hope I have rectified all the errors of my working out and/or the occasional misprints and misinterpretations.

A book gives me the opportunity to explain in full how I arrive at the answers and an insight into the devious paths to the solutions, rather than just giving the simple one-word answers.

I have attempted to include puzzles which are dead-easy and others that will keep the ardent solvers burning the midnight oil. But then, of course, it depends on what you think is easy.

Clive Doig, 1990.

PUZZLES

1 STRIPS

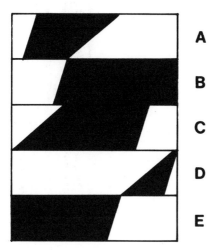

How many of these strips do you have to move to make a regular pattern?

2 TURN OVER

Put four coins down in a row, all heads up.
Turn over one of the coins.
Turn over the one next to it.
Move the inside two to the outside without turning them over.
Turn over both an end one and a middle that are not lying next to each other.

Which of the combinations below could you have arrived at?

a THTH **b** HHHH **c** TTTH **d** HTHT

3 NAMES

One of these anagrams is not a girl's name. Which one is it?

PARTSKINT TWEGHNY RAVE READASELM
SADDENEMO HETERANKI

4 STRAIGHT LINES

Using only straight lines, no curved ones, what is the least number of straight lines you need to draw all 26 letters of the alphabet so that they can be recognisably differentiated? (Try it with matchsticks.)

5 GIRLFRIENDS

Who is who?

Arabella has not got curly hair.
Belinda has not got a big mouth.
Cordelia is not cross-eyed.
Daphne has not got boss eyes.
Enid has got bunches.
Fiona has got normal eyes.
Cordelia is not next to Enid, but Belinda is next to Fiona.

6 GIRLS

Can you pair all the girls' names on the left with the words on the right?

April	Fly
Carol	Coin
Coral	Colour
Daisy	Expectation
Dawn	Flower
Georgia	Fruit
Hope	Happiness
Joy	Jewel
May	Month
Olive	Rock
Penny	Song
Ruby	Sunrise
Violet	US state

7 SIGNS

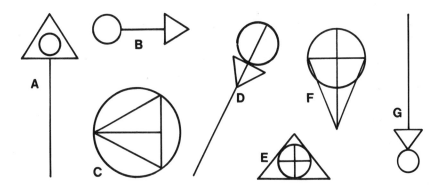

Which is the odd one out?

8 ONE TO FIVE

Insert any of the mathematical symbols + − × ÷ and/or () anywhere between or in front of the numbers to make the sum correct.

$$1\ 2\ 3\ 4\ 5 = 1\ 2$$

9 ONE TO FIVE AGAIN

Follow the instructions for puzzle 8 (above).

$$1\ 2\ 3\ 4\ 5 = 3\ 0$$

10 MORE SUMS

How many different whole positive numbers can you fill in on the right-hand side of the equation, using the symbols and brackets as in puzzle 8 (above)?

$$1\ 2\ 3\ 4\ 5 = ?$$

11 SEQUENCE

What is the next letter in this sequence?

$$E\ Q\ U\ -$$

TRACKWORDS

How many words of three letters or more can you find by tracking from one square to the next; going up, down, sideways or diagonally in order?

You may not go through the same letter square again in one word. No plurals (with an added s), proper nouns or foreign words are allowed.

What is the nine-letter word that can be extracted by tracking through all the letters of the grid?

12

H	E	R
E	A	P
N	D	P

Average score: 35 words
Brainbox score: 56 words

13

C	U	B
C	A	R
N	E	E

Average score: 25 words
Brainbox score: 45 words

14

C	L	E
E	A	B
T	E	R

Average score: 49 words
Brainbox score: 79 words

15 HIDDEN WORD

Starting at the top left-hand corner and reading through all the letters of the grid across, up or down, answer the question:

W	H	A	T	?	S	R
O	E	H	I	T	T	E
N	E	T	S	E	L	X
O	W	E	T	H	A	I
R	I	D	H	H	S	S
D	S	S	I	C	I	H
I	N	G	R	I	D	W

12

16 MUSEUM

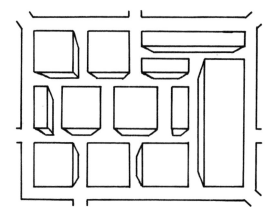

The plan view of the museum room above shows a number of display cabinets.

Can you enter the room and exit, passing each cabinet on at least two sides without going over the same path twice?

17 CONNECTIONS

Find the words which connect the three words and then find the word that connects these three words.

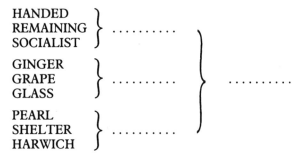

HANDED
REMAINING
SOCIALIST
} . . . .

GINGER
GRAPE
GLASS
} . . . . } . . . .

PEARL
SHELTER
HARWICH
} . . . .

18   COUNTING THE PIPS

In a standard pack of 52 English playing cards the value of each card and its suit symbol is printed on two of the card's corners. How many spade, heart, diamond and club symbols are there altogether in a full pack? (Discount symbols which appear in the costumes of the royal cards and count the aces' motifs as one symbol.)

19   BUNNY

What Easter item do the 11 letters that make up the bunny spell out?

20   EASTER THINGS

Take the last letter of the Eastery answers to the quiz below and spell out a word. What is it?

1   Chocolate or fowl ovoid.
2   Floats and bands and displays.
3   What the bunny spells in no. 19.
4   It comes to an end at Easter.
5   Upon which a cross was set up.
6   Not a bad friend of Robinson Crusoe.

21 SQUARES

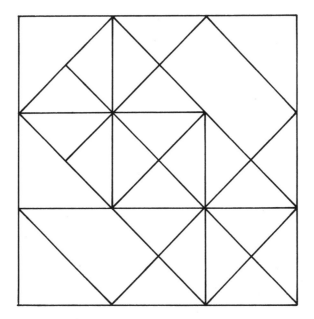

How many squares are there in this diagram?

22 SCORES AND DOZENS

'A score and a half, less half a score and half a half a score' is equal to which of the following?

a   A score, less a dozen and a half
b   A dozen, less half a dozen and a half
c   A score, less half a score and a half
d   A dozen and a half, less half a dozen

TRACKWORDS

How many words of three letters or more can you find by tracking from one square to the next; going up, down, sideways or diagonally in order?

You may not go through the same letter square again in one word. No plurals (with an added s), proper nouns or foreign words are allowed.

What is the nine-letter word that can be extracted by tracking through all the letters of the grid?

23

Y	O	D
R	I	R
O	T	M

Average score: 11 words
Brainbox score: 18 words

24

V	E	N
I	A	G
N	G	R

Average score: 28 words
Brainbox score: 46 words

25

M	E	C
E	O	R
A	T	F

Average score: 30 words
Brainbox score: 56 words

26 SUNRISE

Where in the world can you see the sun rise twice in 24 hours?

27 COUNTIES

There are three English counties jumbled up below. What are they?

DAUIRRHBAMMUCNUOMRBTRHELNDA

28 MIRRORED TILES

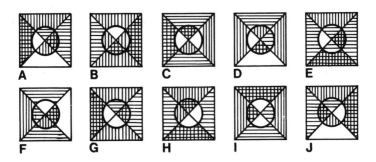

Five pairs of tiles are pictured here. Which pair is the identical pair? How are the other four pairs matched up?

29 PLAYING WITH ACRONYMS

In the small country of PAWBALAND (Place Abounding With Beauty And Love And Nice Dreams) the five major political parties represented in parliament are the:

SWEET (Social Welfare Egalitarian Environment Trust)
CON (Conniving Oligarchy Nationalists)
SHIM (Supremely Happy Idiotic Movement)
LOBBO (Lazy Old Boring Bureaucratic Organisation)
TERROR (Tyrannical Eugenic Rich Rulers Of Royalists)
and there is one
INDEPENDENT member

The difference between the numbers of representatives of each of the five major parties is the same.
There are more SHIM members than CON's in the parliament; and the same number more of LOBBO than TERROR M.P.s.
The coalition of the two largest parties, SWEET and LOBBO holds a majority of one in parliament. All 16 members of the SHIM party are illiterate.

What is the total number of M.P.s in the PAWBALAND parliament and what could INDEPENDENT, as an acronym, stand for?

30 BOX

Look at this box with letters printed on each side. If you find the right letters which replace the question marks in each of the drawings, you will find out what sort of box it is.

NUMBERS AND LETTERS

What expressions, phrases or sayings are represented by these numbers and letters? A number stands for a number, a capital letter is the initial letter of a word.

31 3 B M, 3 B M

32 12 M in the Y

33 7 B for 7 B

34 9 L of a C

35 29 D of F in a L Y

36 18 H of a G C

37 11 P in a F T

38 10 G B K on a W

39 4 S of the Y

40 A B and the 40 T

41 101 D

42 4 P for a T

43 The 4 M M

44 S a S of 6 P

45 A S in T S 9

46 The 10 C

47 3 P for a W, 1 for a D

48 CHRISTMAS THINGS

The last letter of some of these objects can be used to spell out two of the others. Another word is spelled out by the last letters of those remaining. What is it?

49 MANHOLES

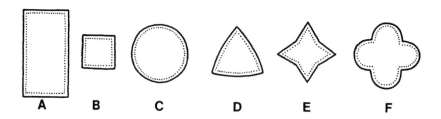

A   B   C   D   E   F

Here are a number of manhole-cover shapes. The dotted lines indicate the hole over which the cover fits. In each case the thickness of the cover is thinner than the overlap. How many of these covers could not fall into their own holes?

TRACKWORDS

How many words of three letters or more can you find by tracking from one square to the next; going up, down, sideways or diagonally in order?

You may not go through the same letter square again in one word. No plurals (with an added s), proper nouns or foreign words are allowed.

What is the nine-letter word that can be extracted by tracking through all the letters of the grid?

50

G	T	S
Y	A	I
M	N	C

Average score: 33 words
Brainbox score: 58 words

51

D	H	A
E	U	R
G	N	A

Average score: 21 words
Brainbox score: 33 words

52

T	A	F
U	I	N
A	T	E

Average score: 14 words
Brainbox score: 28 words

53 ANAGRAMS

Work out the anagrams from the clues:

HANG A FAST IN	A country
GRUBNITS	Exploding
ADJICHEK	Captured
HI DESIGN	Boats
I FEED IN TIN	Not distinguished
PIANO VERITE	Not working
DRIED BUST	Woken up
DICK BACH	A bird
MEAN AMONG	Famous person

All the answers to the nine anagrams above have something in common.
What is it?

54 SHAPES

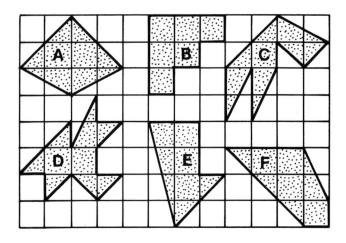

Which of the shapes drawn on the graph paper is the odd one out?

55   TRICKY TRIANGLES

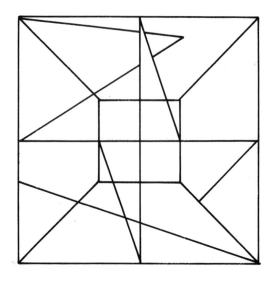

How many triangles are there in this diagram?

EXPRESSIBLES

What are the expressions or phrases represented by these diagrams?

56

57 DOWN

58

D A K E D

59

APPLE

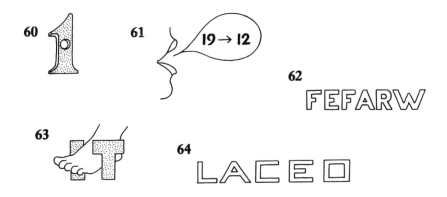

60

61

62

63

64

65 SHOPPING LIST

I went shopping and bought myself a dam. Later I bought some pies and annas. Then I bought some plack, a unicorn and a white eagle. I couldn't leave without some sequins and a quetzal.

What was I doing and where did I buy them? How many countries did they come from?

66 BLOBS

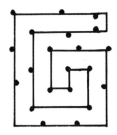

Which blob is the logical start to this diagram?

Clue: start on the outside.

67 JUST FOR STARTERS

How many mammals can you find starting words below?

At the zoo restaurant a customer kept complaining. The catering manager shrewdly assured the dogmatic fellow that every molecule of his aperitif was drinkable. He was rather foxed, however, by the cowardly antics of his bearded waiter who staged a battle with the slothful waitress over who should serve the pigeon pie. The pie was excellent, sealed with a coating of meat glaze and the customer wolfed the lot happily.

68 CARD GAMES

Work out the mixed-up card games below and the last letters will spell out the colour on the back of my pack of cards.

ASCANTA SPAN PERKO BRIGBACE QUIETP TWISH MYRUM GARB FRIENDHEMEC TENPIACE QUIZBEE ONTOPNO

69 STRANGE CROSSES

A LIGER is a cross between a lion and a tiger, and a SHEAT is a cross between a sheep and a goat. Using the same principles, what different animals are the following unlikely crosses between?

DEBRA MOURE BENGO ZENDA MOMEL KOAMA BOAMA ORENA IBUNK HORNK WHALF

70 *DDLE

What are the 15 different 'ddle' words marked * in this story?

I didn't want to *ddle, but Molly had got in a *ddle when she tried to *ddle the pony's *ddle.

'Use your *ddle,' I said. 'It's really a *ddle. Put your bottom in the *ddle.'

'Don't talk *ddle, and don't *ddle me,' said Molly. 'Just *ddle off, OK?'

She had a *ddle with her stirrups, the pony trod in a *ddle and Molly fell off. I rushed up and gave her a *ddle.

'Just *ddle,' she said. 'I have to go through all this just for your stupid *ddle.'

71 PASSWORDS

Complete the different words marked * in this story:

I have a PASS* for travel, so I was looking forward to my PASS* to Australia. If only I hadn't lost my PASS* when I was in India last year. I had to find a PASS* photograph of myself which I keep between the pages of my PASS* for safe keeping. Only then could I become a PASS* on the ship.

72 PEN AND PAPER

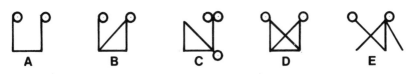

Which of these shapes cannot be drawn without taking the pen off the paper or retracing your steps?

73 INTERTWINABLES

The answers to the first two clues, intertwined, give the answer to the third clue.

Example: What you try to do to a snooker ball *and* What you need after exercise = An objection.
Answer: POT and REST, intertwined, give PROTEST.

Try these intertwinables:

a   A tender or painful spot *and* What cows chew = Scrubbed.

b   Growing woody things *and* The place where you live = Trio.

c   To successfully search for *and* To depend on = Amicable.

74 MORE INTERTWINABLES

The answers to the first two clues, intertwined, give the answer to the last clue.

a Teapot end *and* Pillar box colour = Produced shoots.

b Part played by actor *and* But, it's a bath = To annoy.

c An Eastern chief *and* Garden entrance = To leave to live in.

TRACKWORDS

How many words of three letters or more can you find by tracking from one square to the next; going up, down, sideways or diagonally in order?

You may not go through the same letter square again in one word. No plurals (with an added s), proper nouns or foreign words are allowed.

What is the nine-letter word that can be extracted by tracking through all the letters of the grid?

75
X	U	J
T	O	E
A	P	S

Average score: 21 words
Brainbox score: 36 words

76
K	A	K
W	E	I
I	T	T

Average score: 10 words
Brainbox score: 15 words

77
G	O	L
M	A	I
H	T	R

Average score: 40 words
Brainbox score: 64 words

78 CHRISTMAS POEM

What do we vote with
And send with our love?
The ape without it would not be alone,
Three of them make 100, eight of them a lot;
Yet one is only ten!
But here marks the spot.
Six is back with it, though that must be wrong
Past presidents, girlfriends and boyfriends
All have it, now gone.
If Anne gets it, she's in another wing
For breakfast we have it, Cockney rhymers sing.
It is missing from the man from Man
And it stands for Christ
Now get it if you can.

79 DEBTS

Alan was owed £1 by Betty and then paid off his debt to Carol which now meant that she had twice as much as Betty, who had twice as much as Alan. They each started with an equal amount in pounds. What was it?

80 STARS OF WIMBLEDON

Twenty-five well-known tennis stars, past and present, are hidden in this strange tale. Can you find them all?

'You never try and play canasta,' Senta, the Viking slave, reminded her bored lord and master at the Roman court, as he again shuffled the cards into a neat wad, eagerly dealing them round the game circle for another round of snap. 'Let's try.'

'Who adds up the winnings?' asked Lady Jo, nestling her cash in her lap.

'I'm not going to lend lots of money to anyone,' Lord Eric grumbled. 'I think the game's a con, Norsegirl. I wanted a superb orgy instead.'

'Oh dear, now I land Eric in trouble,' Senta thought.

'Coo,' perked up the lord. 'Give us some perry and let's eat. Serve us a bat in ice, imbue now in spiced bergamot oil and stuff it with hips of rose, wallowing in their own goo.'

'La gong 'as already rung for the nine o'clock orgy, sire,' the slavegirl said in her best French accent.

'Do not say nine, please. IX as in Roman it is. Look at the clock,' the monarch angrily exclaimed.

'Flipping heck,' Senta sighed. 'It's all graft, isn't it?'

81 A STRANGE TOURNAMENT

It was extraordinary at the Mathematicians' Tennis Club. In the men's singles knockout championship all the matches were settled in exactly four sets, and in every match the loser won more games overall than his opponent. All the possible different scores that could occur did, without any two being the same. How many men played in the tournament? Naturally the tie-breaker came into operation at 6-6.

82 KEEPING UP WITH THE JONESES

There are four married couples living in my road called Jones. Judy is Jay's sister (she didn't have to change her name when she got married).

All eight Joneses' ages differ from each other by the same number of years. And the combined ages of each couple add up to the number of their house.

Joel, who is 42, is not married to Jean. Joann is 12 years older than her husband. James lives at No. 108. Can you now work out the Christian name of the man who has not been mentioned, is married to Judith and lives at No. 138? And who live at No. 96?

83 COUNTRIES WITHIN

Inside each of these countries there is a four-letter country hiding anagrammatically – more than one in a couple of cases, but the total you are looking for is 15, one from each. They include islands and an old name.

Malawi   Libya   Ireland   Equatorial Guinea
Upper Volta   Surinam   Somalia   Dutch Guiana
Manchuria   Baluchistan   Eritrea   Guatemala   Monaco   Tobago
Jugoslavia

84 FIREWORKS

I bought a box of 50 fireworks but it was short. I counted a different number of each type of firework. There were four times as many bangers as fizzers, three times as many cracklers as boomers, and twice as many whizzers as boomers. Unfortunately two of each type proved to be duds. This meant that twice as many bangers went off as cracklers, and twice as many sparklers as whizzers. More boomers were dud than went off. How many fizzers were there in the box?

85 COME DANCING

Can you find the 30 different types of dance from the cryptic clues below?
The dances are in order except one. Which is the odd dance out?

1 Type of saw.
2 Rebel without a core.
3 A type of dot.
4 A tot half-way through the ball.
5 University College is without its ancient harp.
6 Brown and green light.
7 Twits turning.
8 Disney to the last letter.
9 Twice able.
10 A minute change.
11 A driven minor.
12 Father and the vehicle go east.
13 Capital, possibly missing the same as its country – Maa.
14 A jacket-like bodice, short of the waist.
15 Stands for F with Charlie.
16 Gave out an 'over the top' order.
17 Top west mix-up.
18 And in rheumatic relieving clay from Battaglio's thermal springs.
19 Hope about the Royal Navy and 3.142.
20 Tea thrice.
21 Churned butter inside 1.
22 Loop beads around.
23 Singer, once with a Mann.
24 A woman's bodice and skirt in one piece, in Scotland but Polish.
25 Lobster dance.
26 A fast pace.
27 The country's heir not back yet.
28 Valley of the Spey.
29 Spider dance.
30 To and fro and over and over.

86 G AND S

The following are cryptic clues to G and S operettas: solve them and then make a word from the first letters (ignoring definite articles).

1 Change the maid, OK?
2 Produced from elation and rugby post.
3 People who died around a twisted idol.
4 The queen's flag and a cry on the golf course.
5 A hat surrounded a dozen peers.
6 A key sign of the heartless gnu inside 3 feet.

87 MORE G AND S

Which is the odd one out in this HAMSUCK and NIMMAJOR list of coded characters. BANG KING, TETE, BEEG SOG, PATOZE, FOLT BEARK, DIP DIP, RORTA BEE and TOKANGO. The same letter substitutions occur throughout.

88 VEG.

Fill the gaps with 17 vegetables:

(   ) weather during the Ladies' Bowls All-Scandinavian Final meant that Kirsten, the Dane, 'Champion of the (   )', did not (   ) Erika, the (   ). Although everyone was frozen to the (   ) and both (-   ) were so cold that they could not grip the bowls, it was Kirsten's shoe springing a (   ) and irritating the (   ) on her foot that really put paid to her chances. With her (   ) racing and her temperature rising, she returned to the (   ) Hotel, where she had (   ) staying. She was dismayed to hear that many other chilblains and hardpads could continue to (   ) up all over her feet.
'That'(   ), as far as bowling's concerned,' advised her coach and nasty husband.
'(   ) think of some other (   ) to enable you to exploit your underarm physical skills, as there is not (   ) left for anything cerebral in that (   ) brain of yours.'

The veg. include bad puns and bad spelling.

TRACKWORDS

How many words of three letters or more can you find by tracking from one square to the next; going up, down, sideways or diagonally in order?

You may not go through the same letter square again in one word. No plurals (with an added s), proper nouns or foreign words are allowed.

What is the nine-letter word that can be extracted by tracking through all the letters of the grid?

89

Y	A	M
F	O	E
L	R	W

Average score: 26 words
Brainbox score: 39 words

90

T	U	N
R	E	N
M	I	T

Average score: 43 words
Brainbox score: 63 words

91

T	S	B
I	O	E
N	A	T

Average score: 33 words
Brainbox score: 58 words

92 WORD CHAIN

By changing one letter at a time, but not altering the order of the letters, can you change CHIME into BELLS, going through CLOCK and without using the same word twice? Perhaps 15 stages are needed.

93 TWO OUT OF THREE

Which of these combinations of two letters do you think start most three-letter words?

BO   BU   DA   KE   LE   MO   SI   TA

94 OH DOAR!

As oou oan oee, oy poinoer oepoacos eoero thord oetoer oito tho leoteo 'o'. How mony oifoeront oetoero haoe boen oepoacod?

95 MUSICAL SEQUENCES

What do the question marks stand for in the following musical sequences?

1   D, R, M, F, S, L, ?, ?
2   H, D, S, Q, C, M, S, ?, ?
3   21, 36, 55, 60, 67, 68, 92, ?, ?
4   U, U, U, U, D, D, D, U, U, D, D, U, D D, ?, ?
5   From She I Can't A I Ticket ? ?

96   moNOpoly

It's said that when Charles Darrow first offered Monopoly to the Parker Brothers in the 1930s they rejected it on 42 counts – perhaps something like this:

> Dear Mr Darrow,
> The latest game you have submitted will n–– take off, n–– in it is good gamesplay, n–– even the buying of property, which n–– of us can afford today. We therefore have to say n–– to your application. We apologise for this n–– reply, but we r–– your claim that the game is interesting, and d–– you any advance. Your chances of making a success with Monopoly are n––, and our previous agreement is now n–– and v––, and is worth n––.
> Yours 'no'ingly, The Parker Brothers.

How wrong they were – though they did change their minds later. Fill in the 12 different negative words.

97   PARTS OF YOU

a   What part of your body could have a wash, wave, storm and a child?
b   What part of your body goes in front of a bag, dive, gay and your face?
c   What part of your body has a bag, book, cuff, stand and some?
d   What part of your body has a pit, chair, a dillo and our plate?

EXPRESSIBLES

What are the expressions or phrases represented by these diagrams?

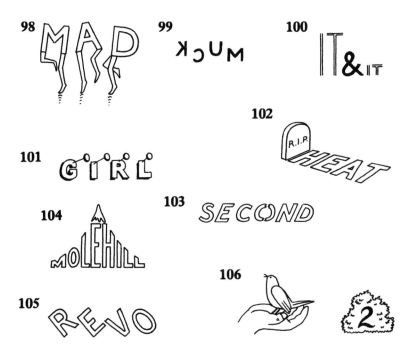

98

99 ᴋ ɔ U ᴍ

100 ‖ T & ɪᴛ

102 R.I.P. HEAT

101 G I R L

103 SECOND

104 MOLEHILL

105 REVO

106

107 IN COMMON

What have the numbers 3, 7, 8, 40, 50, and 60 in common that no other whole numbers have?

108 MORE IN COMMON

What have trousers, braces, knickers, underpants and spectacles in common that socks do not?

109 TEN 0s

Can you match each abbreviation with its 'O' word?

AWOL COI DSO KO MOT OAP OED PTO STOPP VTOL

Of, Off, Office, Official, Old, Opposed, Order, Out, Over, Oxford

110 KNOW HOW

You 'know' it is interesting 'how' the letters 'ow' can be pronounced differently. I compiled a list of all words I could think of ending in 'ow' – there were 113 of them. Which ending do you think is the most common, that of 'know' or that of 'how'?

111 SOUND-ALIKES

Which letter and number sound like words that mean:

1 In front of
2 Struck
3 A Middle Eastern country
4 Kind and mild
5 Devoured
6 Anticipate

For example, 'doglike' would be K9 (canine).

112 LMNTRE

What two letters and a number sound like words that mean:

1 Temporary occupation
2 To flow forth
3 To navigate the air

For example, 'diverge' would be DV8 (deviate).

113 ONLY LETTERS

What three letters sound like or nearly sound like the words described below?

1 Prettiness
2 A foe
3 Joyful feeling
4 An American state
5 Something measured in joules
6 To make a god of

For example, a likeness would be FEG (effigy)

114 FOUR-LETTER WORDS

In each case below, what four letters sound like words that mean:

1 A place where bees are kept
2 Great merit
3 The state of being an idiot
4 Effectiveness
5 A large cage for birds
6 A high-ranking official

115 FIRST TEST

After the first Test between Westland and Engindies it was noted that during their first innings Engindies had bowled at precisely 15 overs an hour, scored at exactly 4 runs an over and lost a wicket after every 8 overs. Westland had bowled at a rate of 18 overs an hour, scored at 3 runs an over and lost a wicket after every 10 hours.

In the second innings, however, Westland put their run rate up to 3.5 runs an over and both teams improved their loss-of-wickets average by 1 over per wicket, though their batting rates remained the same.

There had been exactly four-and-a-half hours' play possible on each of the five days, plus an allocated extra 18 overs on the last day. Engindies won the toss and put Westland in to bat.

What was the result?

116 INITIALLY

Can you work out who the people are described below?

1 Specially useful person easily rectifies many alien nasties.
2 Cherished lovely Egyptian of pharaoh ancestry totally ruined Antony.
3 Jewish emissary sold us selflessness; could he raise interest selling today?
4 Chinese orator now fabled uttered commonly ingenious useful sayings.
5 Marvellous adventurer reaches China; orders peppermints of lovely Orient.
6 Cunning loony is very evil, delving openly in guesswork.

Try it with your own name or that of friends and foes.

117 BOB A JOB

The bob, or shilling, is equal to 5p – or, rather, it was when Britain went decimal in 1971. Do you know some other names for old money?
Clues below:

1 Robert for short.
2 Someone who tans leather.
3 A guilder.
4 Used to go with a penny to make a velocipede.
5 Something like an octopus with an initial shilling missing.
6 Half of what the queen can wear on her head.
7 An equatorial African country.

Now find what each of them was worth in decimal currency and add them up. (You'll need some help.) What is the total value of coins 1 to 7, to the nearest tenth of a new penny? Most of the names of the above are no longer in everyday use. Which is the odd one out?

118 ARMADAS

How many Armadas can you find forwards and backwards in the mad little conflict described below?

'You're very aggressive,' his mum said to him as Adam raised his arm. 'A dastardly, vulgar, mad and silly thing to do as it could alarm Ada, the maid.' Adam didn't care. Rather than exonerating himself by saying, 'War, madam, rarely solves problems,' he said to his dear ma, 'dad hated armed conflict. He never did anyone any harm, adapting his belligerence for peace. Didn't he lose all his hair in the war?' 'Madarosis, that was!,' his mother snapped. 'My dear, mad Adam it's time you went home,' and she lovingly clouted him over the head with her stick. 'Ada, Mr Adamant is leaving!' 'Let go of my arm, Ada!' Adam whined as he was frog-marched away.

119 THE ALBUM PAGE

I collect cheese labels. I have recently acquired seven very rare labels from Zblogovia, which I want to stick on a single page in my album. The page measures 13 cm × 20 cm and I would like a gap of 1 cm between each label and between the labels and the edge of the page. Six of the labels measure as follows: 11 × 4 cm, 9 × 4 cm, 7 × 3 cm, 5 × 2 cm, 3 × 3 cm, 3 × 2 cm. If they all fitted on the page with exactly 1 cm gap between each, what was the largest possible size of the seventh?

120 EXAM RESULTS

My mathematically-minded mate, Matthew Mather, and I got the same number of GCSE passes. Afterwards he gloomily said to me: 'Do you know that I sat one more exam than Robert, who sat one more than Elaine, but she passed one more than he did, and he passed one more than I did. Between the three of us we passed exactly two thirds of all the subjects we took.'

'Good Heavens,' I said. 'Precisely the same thing happened to me, Mary and Susan. Though poor old Susan failed more than she passed.'

How many passes did Elaine get? Did any one of the six of us pass all the exams they took?

121 COLOURFUL MARRIAGES

White's brother married Lemon's husband's sister.
Brown did not marry Green.
Black did not marry Green.
There used to be more Greens than any other colour, and since they got married there still are.
Mrs Brown is called Yolande.
There are eight people. Who married whom?

122 DOG QUIZ

Identify the following breeds:

Long-haired sheepdog.
Like a King Charles.
Sledge puller.
Fred.
Very small Mexican dog.
Racing dog.

Take the third letter of each answer: a canine star appears.

123 SIMPLE SUMS

Insert any of the following signs between any numbers on the left of the equations to make them correct. You may join numbers on the left together if you wish: e.g., 3 6 may become 36.

The signs you may use are $+$, $-$, $\times$, $\div$, and ( )

1   4 1 4 3 = 111
2   5 9 5 3 = 222
3   4 8 5 7 = 333

TRACKWORDS

How many words of three letters or more can you find by tracking from one square to the next; going up, down, sideways or diagonally in order?

You may not go through the same letter square again in one word. No plurals (with an added s), proper nouns or foreign words are allowed.

What is the nine-letter word that can be extracted by tracking through all the letters of the grid?

124

P	E	D
S	O	U
M	Y	N

Average score: 26 words
Brainbox score: 47 words

125

T	E	Q
R	R	U
L	Y	A

Average score: 13 words
Brainbox score: 19 words

126

E	B	R
R	A	P
Y	R	S

Average score: 30 words
Brainbox score: 45 words

127 QUIZZLE

Who are these famous birthday people? The last letters of their names can be rearranged to make a number.

29 April 1895: Knighted English conductor, almost also an NCO.

30 April 1777: The cgs unit magnetic flux density is named after this German mathematician.

1 May 1672: Founder of the *Spectator*, English essayist and creator of the opera *Rosamund*.

2 May 1859: English humorous writer who had two names the same and a middle name of Klapka.

3 May 1469: 'The most evil rulers' actions can be justified by the wickedness and treachery of those governed.' So he said and gave his name to such thinking.

4 May 1769: English portraitist, famous for his full-length portrait of Queen Charlotte. Not of Arabia.

5 May 1818: German founder of international communism, but not one of the brothers. Buried in Highgate.

TRACKWORDS

How many words of three letters or more can you find by tracking from one square to the next; going up, down, sideways or diagonally in order?

You may not go through the same letter square again in one word. No plurals (with an added s), proper nouns or foreign words are allowed.

What is the nine-letter word that can be extracted by tracking through all the letters of the grid?

128

S	C	N
E	A	E
M	B	L

Average score: 41 words
Brainbox score: 71 words

129

T	N	G
A	R	I
M	P	L

Average score: 50 words
Brainbox score: 78 words

130

R	E	N
V	U	D
E	S	T

Average score: 31 words
Brainbox score: 55 words

131   A MONTH OF BIRTHDAYS

Who (or what) was born on the following days?

1 January 1854: The studies of early superstition, religious beliefs and society in *The Golden Bough* were written by someone born on New Year's Day.

2 January 1905: Born in London, this English composer is a dedicated pacifist who was imprisoned for three months during the Second World War as a conscientious objector. Who is this composer of the operas *The Midsummer Marriage* and *King Priam* who was knighted in 1966?

3 January 1909:   Who is the comedian born in Denmark on this day? Famous for his puns at the piano, he was once allowed to overrun by 20 minutes on his own special TV show for the BBC.

4 January 1809:   A Frenchman who at the age of three became blind and went on to invent a system that enabled the blind to read and write.

5 January 1938:   A European king. He has been king of his country for only 13 years, but 'pretending' for much longer.

6 January 1956:   Happy Birthday to an actress who had her film debut in *My Teenage Daughter*, but is perhaps most famed for her leading role in *Ice Cold in Alex*.

7 January 1899:   The composer of *Les Biches*, born in France. Pronounced 'onk' and 'ank'! Who was he?

8 January 1935:   Surviving twin born this day became greatest Memphis rock star. Who was he?

9 January 1913:   Happy Birthday to the Watergate president. Who is that?

10 January 1843:   Although his notorious brother Jesse was murdered, this man survived a murder trial. Who was he?

11 January 1858:   Who, born on this day, founded the first American-style store in England on London's Oxford Street in 1909?

12 January 1729:   Born in Dublin. Although an eloquent literary Whig opposed to North, he became one of the great influences on modern Conservative philosophy. Who?

13 January 1918:   The creator of *Dixon of Dock Green*, who became a lord. Who is he?

14 January 1904:   A British knighted photographer and designer: *My Fair Lady* among others.

15 January 1918:   Egyptian leader, 1954–1970.

16 January 1929:   One has been able to speak to this periodically, from this day in 1929 to today.

17 January 1899:   Born in Brooklyn, notorious in Chicago. Only ever sentenced to prison for tax evasion.

18 January 1904:   British Hollywood actor. He was Archibald Leach then.

19 January 1809: An American poet. Before he died at 40 he had written many weird and often horrible stories that still delight us.

20 January 1934: Count through the Doctor Whos that have appeared on BBC tv. This one was forth.

21 January 1824: A confederate general known as Stonewall.

22 January 1788: A lordly poet.

23 January 1719: A tiny principality on the Rhine founded on this day.

24 January 1924: The Prince of Wales's father-in-law.

25 January 1874: Born on Burns Day, a British writer famed for his short stories and novels. *Rain* and *The Moon and Sixpence* are among his greats.

26 January 1928: Husky-voiced American singer who starred in the film *New Faces*.

27 January 1924: Happy Birthday to the knight of Whitehall farce fame who has done so much for MENCAP.

28 January 1929: The famous clarinettist who made *Stranger on the Shore* a hit.

29 January 1939: An Australian feminist, originator of *The Female Eunuch*.

30 January 1882: The American president who saw the start, but not the end, of the Second World War.

31 January 1797: An Austrian composer who wanted to know who Sylvia was and left his eighth symphony unfinished.

TRACKWORDS

How many words of three letters or more can you find by tracking from one square to the next; going up, down, sideways or diagonally in order?

You may not go through the same letter square again in one word. No plurals (with an added s), proper nouns or foreign words are allowed.

What is the nine-letter word that can be extracted by tracking through all the letters of the grid?

132

R	A	V
L	I	E
U	C	H

Average score: 21 words
Brainbox score: 36 words

133

W	H	I
I	A	T
T	B	E

Average score: 20 words
Brainbox score: 30 words

134

T	E	C
R	O	I
Z	O	P

Average score: 20 words
Brainbox score: 34 words

135 DOMINOES

All dominoes are twice as long as they are wide and there are 28 domino tiles in a set, consisting of seven suits of seven numbers each (a bit of a conundrum in itself). All I want you to do is make letters of the alphabet out of dominoes, or draw them if that's easier, like this:

DOMINO ALPHABET

How many dominoes do you need in total to make all the capital letters of the alphabet, with each letter being exactly the same height? I have done it with 130 dominoes (I drew the letters out). Can you do better?

DOMINO WORD

What is the longest word you can make with one set of 28 dominoes? I made an eight-letter word. Can you do better?

ANSWERS AT A GLANCE

(Those marked * have full explanations or solutions from page 49. The full lists of 'TRACKWORD' words start on page 69.)

1 *3
2 *b HHHH
3 *STINKTRAP
4 *76
5 *Belinda, Fiona, Daphne, Enid, Arabella, Cordelia
6 April   month
    Carol   song
    Coral   rock
    Daisy   flower
    Dawn   sunrise
    Georgia   US state
    Hope   expectation
    Joy   happiness
    May   fly
    Olive   fruit
    Penny   coin
    Ruby   jewel
    Violet   colour
7 *E
8 *(12 + 3) × 4 ÷ 5 = 12
9 *1 + (2 × 3 × 4) + 5 = 30
10 *See 'Full Solutions'
11 *E
12 APPREHEND
13 BUCCANEER
14 CELEBRATE
15 *INSIDE
16 *YES – see 'Full Solutions'
17 *LEFT/WINE/HARBOUR = PORT
18 *348
19 HOT CROSS BUN
20 *GENTLY
21 18
22 *b
23 DORMITORY
24 ENGRAVING

25 FORCEMEAT
26 *Everywhere
27 DURHAM, NORTHUMBERLAND, CUMBRIA
28 G and H – mirror images of each other
29 *81   Independent National Democratic Eccentric Proletariat Environmental Neo-Dadaist Ecological Nostalgic Trend
30 *Shoe
31 3 Blind Mice, 3 Blind Mice
32 12 Months in the Year
33 7 Brides for 7 Brothers
34 9 Lives of a Cat
35 29 Days of February in a Leap Year
36 18 Holes of a Golf Course
37 11 Players in a Football Team
38 10 Green Bottles Hanging on a Wall
39 4 Seasons of the Year
40 Ali Baba and the 40 Thieves
41 101 Dalmatians
42 4 Points for a Try
43 The 4 Minute Mile
44 Sing a Song of 6 Pence
45 A Stitch in Time Saves 9
46 The 10 Commandments
47 3 Points for a Win, 1 for a Draw
48 *DRY
49 *C and D
50 GYMNASTIC

51 HARANGUED
52 INFATUATE
53 *All contain 3 consecutive letters of the alphabet
54 *F
55 17
56 Flash in the pan
57 Down in the mouth
58 Half-baked
59 Apple turnover
60 A hole in one
61 Talk 19 to the dozen
62 Few and far between
63 Put your foot in it
64 Straight-laced
65 *I was buying coins from India, Scotland, the USA, Italy and Guatemala
66 *See 'Full Solutions'
67 *18
68 *A PRETTY GREEN
69 *2 letters at front/3 letters from rear
or
3 letters at front/2 letters from rear
70 *See 'Full Solutions'
71 PASSION, PASSAGE, PASSPORT, PASSABLE, PASSBOOK, PASSENGER
72 E
73 *a SCOURED
b THREESOME
c FRIENDLY
74 *a SPROUTED
b TROUBLE
c EMIGRATE
75 JUXTAPOSE
76 KITTIWAKE
77 LOGARITHM
78 *X
79 *7

80 *There are actually 28
81 *91
82 *Jerome; Joel and Joann live at No. 96
83 MALI, BALI, IRAN, IRAQ, PERU, SIAM, LAOS, CHAD, ANAM, CUBA, EIRE, GUAM, OMAN, TOGO, JAVA
84 *4
85 *Bolero should be between waltz and cancan
86 *MIGHTY
87 *JACK POINT
88 *CHILLI, GREENS, BEET, SWEDE, MARROW, LADIES' FINGERS, LEEK, CORN, PULSE, SAVOY, BEAN, SPROUT, SHALLOT, LETTUCE, CAPER, MUSHROOM, PEA
89 MAYFLOWER
90 NUTRIMENT
91 OBSTINATE
92 CHIME, CHINE, CLINE, CLONE, CLONK, CLOCK, CLICK, CLINK, CHINK, CHINS, COINS, COILS, BOILS, BOLLS, BELLS
93 *TA
94 *15
95 *1 T, D
2 B, L
3 93, 125
4 D, D
5 Help Day
96 never, nothing, not, none, no, negative, reject, deny, nil, null, void, nowt
97 a Brain; b Nose; c Hand; d Arm

98 HOPPING MAD
99 MUCK ABOUT
100 THE LONG AND THE SHORT OF IT
101 PIN-UP GIRL
102 DEAD HEAT
103 SPLIT SECOND
104 MAKE A MOUNTAIN OUT OF A MOLEHILL
105 LEANING OVER BACKWARDS
106 A BIRD IN THE HAND IS WORTH TWO IN THE BUSH
107 *Five letters
108 A pair of them is a single item of clothing
109 Absent without **official** leave
Central **Office** of Information
Distinguished Service **Order**
Knock **out**
Ministry **of** Transport
Old Age Pension(er)
Oxford English Dictionary
Please turn **over**
Society of Teachers
Opposed to Physical Punishment
Vertical Take-**off** and Landing
110 *'ow' as in know
111 *1 B4
2 B10
3 Q8
4 B9
5 E10
6 4C
112 *1 10NC
2 MN8
3 AV8

113 *1 BUT
2 NME
3 XTC
4 IOR
5 NRG
6 DFI
114 *1 APRE
2 XLNC
3 EDOC
4 FEKC
5 AVRE
6 MNNC
115 *Westland won by 5 runs with 1 over to spare
116 *Superman, Cleopatra, Jesus Christ, Confucius, Marco Polo, Clive Doig
117 *1 Bob
2 Tanner
3 Florin
4 Farthing
5 Quid
6 Half a crown
7 Guinea
£2 35.1p
Quid
118 *11 − 9 forwards, 2 backwards
119 *9 cm × 3 cm
120 *Elaine got 7 passes. I passed all I sat
121 *Mr White m. Miss Green
Mr Brown m. Miss Black
Mr Green m. Miss Lemon
Mr Green m. Miss White
122 *Lassie
123 $(41 − 4) \times 3 = 111$
$(5 \times 9 \times 5) − 3 = 222$
$(4 \times 85) − 7 = 333$
124 PSEUDONYM
125 QUARTERLY
126 RASPBERRY
127 *Sixteen

FULL SOLUTIONS

1 STRIPS 3

Remove 'D'. Take out 'B', turn it upside down and put it back where 'D' was. Then turn 'A' upside down and put it where 'B' was. Put 'D' right way up on top.

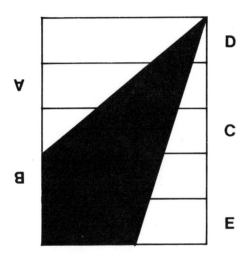

2 TURN OVER HHHH

Starting from HHHH, the only way to arrive at the answer is to turn over an end coin. Then the next one to it giving:
TTHH
Now move the inside two (without turning over) to either end, *crossing them over*!!:
HTHT
The end T and the middle T are now turned over to give:
HHHH

3 NAMES STINKTRAP

The girls' names are: GWYNETH VERA ESMERALDA DESDEMONA and KATHERINE

4 STRAIGHT LINES 76

ABCDEFGHIJKLMN
VPQRSTUVWXYZ

5 GIRLFRIENDS Belinda, Fiona, Daphne, Enid, Arabella, Cordelia

Girl	1	2	3	4	5	6
Hair	CURLY	CURLY	STRAIGHT	BUNCHES	STRAIGHT	BUNCHES
Eyes	CROSS	NORMAL	CROSS	CROSS	BOSS	NORMAL
Mouth	SMALL	BIG	BIG	SMALL	BIG	SMALL
From the information given:						
Arabella			A	A	A	A
Belinda	B			B		B
Cordelia		C			C	C
Daphne	D	D	D	D		D
Enid				E		E
Fiona		F				F

If Belinda is next to Fiona, only 1–B and 2–F comply. Cordelia cannot be no. 5 because she would then be next to Enid (4 or 6). Therefore she must be no. 6 and Enid no. 4. The rest follows:

1	2	3	4	5	6
B	F	D	E	A	C

7 SIGNS E

'E' has an extra straight line – 5 lines. The others have 4 lines.

8   ONE TO FIVE $(12+3)\times4\div5 = 12$

There are many other answers. Here are a few examples:

$$1+2-3+4-5 = 1-2$$
$$-1-2-3+4+5 = 1+2$$
$$1-2+3+4-5 = -1+2$$
$$(1+2+3+4)\div5 = 1\times2$$

9   ONE TO FIVE AGAIN $1+(2\times3\times4)+5 = 30$

Again there are many other solutions, such as:

$$1-2+3-4+5 = 3+0$$
or
$$(1\times2)-3-4+5 = 3\times0$$

10   MORE SUMS   All the numbers to 50 are possible. Here are the first 30:

$1-2+3+4-5 = 1$	$1+(2\times3)+4+5 = 16$
$-(1\times2)+3-4+5 = 2$	$-12+34-5 = 17$
$1-2+3-4+5 = 3$	$-1+(2\times3\times4)-5 = 18$
$1-(2\times3)+4+5 = 4$	$(1\times2)-3+(4\times5) = 19$
$1+2+3+4-5 = 5$	$1+2-3+(4\times5) = 20$
$1-2+(3\times4)-5 = 6$	$-(1\times2)+3+(4\times5) = 21$
$1+2+3-4+5 = 7$	$1-2+3+(4\times5) = 22$
$1+(2\times3)-4+5 = 8$	$1+23+4-5 = 23$
$1+2-3+4+5 = 9$	$-1+2+3+(4\times5) = 24$
$(1+2+3-4)\times5 = 10$	$(1\times2)+3+(4\times5) = 25$
$1-2+3+4+5 = 11$	$-1-2+34-5 = 26$
$(12+3)\times4\div5 = 12$	$1+(2\times3)+(4\times5) = 27$
$-1-(2\times3)+(4\times5) = 13$	$-1+(2\times3\times4)+5 = 28$
$-1-2-3+(4\times5) = 14$	$(1\times2\times3\times4)+5 = 29$
$1+2+3+4+5 = 15$	$1+(2\times3\times4)+5 = 30$

There are many alternatives to the above solutions.

If you are trying to work them all out, don't forget the numbers

$$2345 = 1\times2345$$
$$4140 = 12\times345$$
$$5535 = 123\times45$$
$$6170 = 1234\times5$$
and of course 12345

11 SEQUENCE E

The next letter in 'THIS SEQUENCE'!

15 HIDDEN WORD INSIDE

The sentence in the grid reads:

WHAT IS THE ONE WORD INSIDE THIS GRID WHICH HAS SIX LETTERS?

16 MUSEUM yes

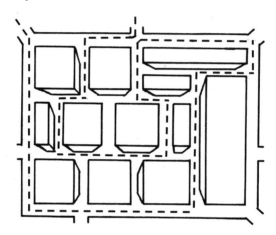

17 CONNECTIONS left/wine/harbour = port

Left-handed/Remaining = Left/Socialist = Left
Ginger wine/Grape wine/Wine glass
Pearl Harbour/Shelter = Harbour/Harwich harbour

Left = Port/Port wine/Harbour = Port

18 COUNTING THE PIPS 348

In each suit: cards ace to 10 have a total of 55 pips
+2×10 symbols in each card's corner = 75.
The jack, queen and king have 2 pips each
+2 in the corners = 4×3 = 12.

Each suit has 87.

Therefore a pack has 4×87 = 348.

20 EASTER THINGS   GENTLY

1 Egg
2 Parade
3 Hot cross bun
4 Lent
5 Calvary Hill
6 Good Friday

22 SCORES AND DOZENS   b

Through different interpretations of 'and a half', the statement: 'A score and a half, less half a score and half a half a score' could equal:

$$20+10-10-5 = 15$$
or $20+\frac{1}{2}-10-5 = 5\frac{1}{2}*$

a   'A score, less a dozen and a half' could equal:

$$20-12-6 = 2$$
or $20-12-\frac{1}{2} = 7\frac{1}{2}$

b   'A dozen, less half a dozen and a half' could equal:

$$12-\frac{1}{2}(12+6) = 3$$
or $12-6-\frac{1}{2} = 5\frac{1}{2}*$

c   'A score, less half a score and a half' could equal:

$$20-\frac{1}{2}(20+10) = 5$$
or $20-10-\frac{1}{2} = 9\frac{1}{2}$

d   'A dozen and a half, less half a dozen' could equal:

$$12+6-6 = 12$$
or $12+\frac{1}{2}-6 = 6\frac{1}{2}$

*$5\frac{1}{2}$ is the only answer which complies with the interpretation of the question and answer b.

26 SUNRISE   Everywhere

If the days are getting longer, as they do everywhere in the world during winter and spring, the sun rises earlier each day: i.e., within 24 hours of its rising the previous day.

29 PLAYING WITH ACRONYMS 81

If SWEET and LOBBO are the two largest parties, and there are more LOBBO than TERROR, and more SHIM than CON, then the order of parties could be as follows:

a SWEET-LOBBO-TERROR-SHIM-CON-INDEPENDENT
b SWEET-LOBBO-SHIM-TERROR-CON-INDEPENDENT
c SWEET-LOBBO-SHIM-CON-TERROR-INDEPENDENT
d LOBBO-SWEET-TERROR-SHIM-CON-INDEPENDENT
e LOBBO-SWEET-SHIM-TERROR-CON-INDEPENDENT
f LOBBO-SWEET-SHIM-CON-TERROR-INDEPENDENT

But LOBBO−TERROR = SHIM−CON
Alternatives c, d, e and f do not comply.
Therefore we can make up the following tables for a and b:

Where 'x' = the difference between the parties

a			b	
SWEET	$= 16+3x$		SWEET	$= 16+2x$
LOBBO	$= 16+2x$		LOBBO	$= 16+x$
TERROR	$= 16+x$	**or**	SHIM	$= 16$
SHIM	$= 16$		TERROR	$= 16-x$
CON	$= 16-x$		CON	$= 16-2x$
INDEPENDENT = 1			INDEPENDENT = 1	

As SWEET+LOBBO = SHIM+CON+TERROR+INDEPENDENT+1

Then in a:
$(16+3x)+(16+2x) = (16+x)+16+(16-x)+1+1$
$32+5x = 50$
$5x = 18$
$x = 3.6$ IMPOSSIBLE

With b:
$(16+2x)+(16+x) = 16+(16-x)+(16-2x)+1+1$
$32+3x = 50-3x$
$6x = 18$
$x = 3$ CORRECT

The numbers of each party must therefore be:

SWEET	22	
LOBBO	19	
SHIM	16	
TERROR	13	
CON	10	
INDEPENDENT	1	LOBBO−TERROR = 6 & SHIM−CON = 6
TOTAL	81	SWEET+LOBBO = 41 A majority of 1 over all other parties

The acronym 'INDEPENDENT' can be made up from any words.
'Independent National Democratic Eccentric Proletariat Environmental Neo-Dadaist Ecological Nostalgic Trend' is only my feeble attempt. Perhaps you can do better!!

30 BOX SHOE

The letters on the box are:

O, N or Z, S, H, C or U and E

48 CHRISTMAS THINGS DRY

The two objects spelled out by the last letter of the others are:

BELL: Crib - Mistletoe - Carol - Tinsel
and TREE: Present - Star - Bauble - Cake

Leaving Card - Cracker - Holly = DRY

49 MANHOLES C and D

In all the other cases there is a shorter width to length or diagonal.

53 ANAGRAMS All contain 3 consecutive letters of the alphabet

AFGHANISTAN
BURSTING
HIJACKED
DINGHIES
INDEFINITE
INOPERATIVE
DISTURBED
DABCHICK
AGAMEMNON

54 SHAPES F

The areas of A, B, C, D and E are all equal to 6 squares on the grid. The area of F is equal to 6½ squares.

65 SHOPPING LIST I was buying coins from India, Scotland, the USA, Italy and Guatemala

A 'dam' is an obsolete Indian copper coin, $\frac{1}{40}$ rupee.
A 'pie' is also from India: withdrawn in 1957, it was equal to $\frac{1}{3}$ of a 'pice' or $\frac{1}{2}$ an 'anna' (see below).
An 'anna' is a coin from India, also obsolete from 1957; it was equal to $\frac{1}{16}$ rupee.
A 'plack' is an old Scottish copper coin, worth $\frac{1}{3}$ of an English old penny.

A 'unicorn' is also Scottish, a gold coin bearing a unicorn and worth 18 Scottish shillings.
A 'white eagle' is a gold coin of 1705 from the USA worth 10 dollars.
A 'sequin' is an old Italian gold coin worth about 46p in English money.
And a 'quetzal' is still the Guatemalan currency unit, now more frequently called a dollar.
I was naturally buying them in a numismatist (coin collector) shop!

66 BLOBS

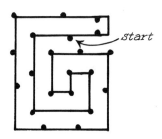

The sequence starts with 1 blob on the outside of the line, then 2 on the inside, 3 on the outside, etc.

67 JUST FOR STARTERS 18

Cat, man, shrew, ass, dog, mole, ape, rat, fox, cow, bear, stag, bat, sloth, pig, seal, coati, wolf.

68 CARD GAMES A PRETTY GREEN

CANASTA, SNAP, POKER, CRIBBAGE, PIQUET, WHIST, RUMMY, BRAG, CHEMIN DE FER, PATIENCE, BEZIQUE, PONTOON

69 STRANGE CROSSES 2 letters at front, 3 letters from rear or 3 letters at front, 2 letters from rear

DEER/ZEBRA, MOUSE/HARE, BEAR/DINGO, ZEBU/PANDA, MOLE/CAMEL, KOALA/PUMA, BOAR/LLAMA, ORYX/HYENA, IBEX/SKUNK, HORSE/MINK, WHALE/WOLF.

70 RIDDLE

Meddle, muddle, straddle, saddle, noddle, doddle, middle, twaddle, mollycoddle, toddle, fiddle, puddle, cuddle, skedaddle, riddle.

73 INTERWINABLES SCOURED – THREESOME – FRIENDLY

a SORE+CUD = SCOURED
b TREES+HOME = THREESOME
c FIND+RELY = FRIENDLY

74 MORE INTERWINABLES SPROUTED – TROUBLE – EMIGRATE

a SPOUT+RED = SPROUTED
b ROLE+TUB = TROUBLE
c EMIR+GATE = EMIGRATE

78 CHRISTMAS POEM X

Vote = X
Kiss = X
ApeX
X × X (Roman numerals) = C or 100
8 Xs (pools)
X = 10 (Roman numerals)
X marks the spot
SiX = 'is' backwards+X
X is wrong
eX presidents, girlfriends and boyfriends
AnneX
X (eggs) for breakfast (Cockney alphabet)
ManX
Xmas = Christmas

79 DEBTS 7

If Alan has £x to start with and £y to finish with, then:

A x becomes y
B x becomes 2y
C x becomes 4y

Therefore 3x = 7y

Also x−1 = 2y
(Betty owes Alan £1, so Betty's x−1 must = 2y)

Multiply by 3:

$$3x = 7y$$
$$3x-3 = 6y$$

Then:

$$3 = y \text{ and } x = 7$$

A £7 becomes £3 – Alan from Betty+£1, Alan to Carol−£5
b £7 becomes £6 – Betty to Alan−£1
c £7 becomes £8 – Carol from Alan+£5

57

80   STARS OF WIMBLEDON   28

Evert, Ryan, Nastase, King, Laver, Court, Ashe, Wade, Mecir, Round, Hoad, Jones, Cash, Pim, Lendl, Connors, Borg, Wilander, Cooper, Perry, Sabatini, Bueno, Edberg, Rosewall, Goolagong, Seixas, Chang, Graf.

81   A STRANGE TOURNAMENT   91

There are 90 different combinations of four games where the loser wins more games than the winner. These are:

0–6	7–6	7–6	7–6	(21–24)	×3
0–6	7–6	7–6	7–5	(21–23)	×3
0–6	7–6	7–5	7–6		×3
0–6	7–5	7–6	7–6		×3
0–6	7–6	7–6	6–4	(20–22)	×3
0–6	7–6	6–4	7–6		×3
0–6	6–4	7–6	7–6		×3
0–6	7–6	7–5	7–5	(21–22)	×3
0–6	7–5	7–6	7–5		×3
0–6	7–5	7–5	7–6		×3
0–6	7–6	7–5	6–4	(20–21)	×3
0–6	7–6	6–4	7–5		×3
0–6	7–5	7–6	6–4		×3
0–6	7–5	6–4	7–6		×3
0–6	6–4	7–6	7–5		×3
0–6	6–4	7–5	7–6		×3
0–6	7–6	6–4	6–4	(19–20)	×3
0–6	6–4	7–6	6–4		×3
0–6	6–4	6–4	7–6		×3
0–6	7–6	7–6	6–3	(20–21)	×3
0–6	7–6	6–3	7–6		×3
0–6	6–3	7–6	7–6		×3
1–6	7–6	7–6	7–6	(22–24)	×3
1–6	7–6	7–6	7–5	(22–23)	×3
1–6	7–6	7–5	7–6		×3
1–6	7–6	7–6	6–4		×3
1–6	7–6	7–6	6–4	(21–22)	×3
1–6	7–6	6–4	7–6		×3
1–6	6–4	7–6	7–6		×3
2–6	7–6	7–6	7–6	(23–24)	×3

(the losing game being the first, second or third)

$$30×3 = 90$$

Therefore, if there were 90 games, there must have been 91 players: 1 winner, 90 losers.

82 KEEPING UP WITH THE JONESES   Jerome; Joel and Joann live at No. 96

The key to this puzzle is that the ages of the people mentioned are determined by the value of the letters in their names: A = 1, B = 2, C = 3, etc.

Therefore:

JOEL	(10+15+5+12)	= 42
JAMES	(10+1+13+5+19)	= 48
JUDY	(10+21+4+25)	= 60
JAY	(10+1+25)	= 36
JEAN	(10+5+1+14)	= 30
JOANN	(10+15+1+14+14)	= 54
JUDITH	(10+21+4+9+20+8)	= 72

The difference between their ages is 6: 30/36/42/48/54/60/—/72

Missing man = 66

JEROME (10+5+18+15+13+5) = 66 fits; so do a number of other names, but maybe not beginning with J!!!

James, 48, lives with Judy 60 at No. 108
Judith, 72, lives with (Jerome), 66, at No. 138
Jay (who must be a man), 36, lives with Jean, 30, at No. 60
and Joel, 42, lives with Joann, 54, at No. 96

84 FIREWORKS   4

If two of each firework were dud and more boomers were dud than went off, there must have been either (a) no boomers or (b) one boomer that went off.

(a)

		Went off		Total bought
Boomers		0	+2	2
Whizzers	(2×Boomers)	2	+2	4
Cracklers	(3×Boomers)	4	+2	6
Sparklers	(2×Whizzers)	4	**Wrong! Because no fireworks had the same number**	

	Went off		Total bought
Boomers	1	+2	3
Whizzers	4	+2	6 (2×Boomers)
Cracklers	7	+2	9 (3×Boomers)
Sparklers	8 (2×Whizzers)	+2	10
Bangers	14 (2×Cracklers)	+2	16 (4×Fizzers)
Fizzers	2	+2	4
Totals	36		48 in box (2 short)

85 COME DANCING Bolero should be between waltz and cancan

1 Jig
2 Reel (Rebel)
3 Polka
4 Rumba (rum+ba)
5 Samba (Sambuca)
6 Tango (tan+go)
7 Twist
8 Waltz (Walt+z)
9 Cancan (can can)
10 Minuet
11 Morris
12 Pavane (Pa+van+E)
13 Valeta (Valletta – capital of Malta)
14 Bolero
15 Foxtrot
16 Gavotte (Gave+OTT)
17 Two-step
18 Fandango (and+fango)
19 Hornpipe (Hope+RN + pi)
20 Cha-cha-cha
21 Jitterbug (Butter+jig [answer 1])
22 Paso doble
23 Paul Jones (former lead singer with Manfred Mann)
24 Polonaise
25 Quadrille
26 Quickstep
27 Charleston (Charles+not)
28 Strathspey
29 Tarantella
30 Rock 'n' roll (rock and roll)

The order in which the dances have been placed is according to the number of letters in the words and then alphabetically. Bolero (six letters) should be between waltz (five) and cancan (six).

86 G AND S MIGHTY

1 *The Mikado* (anagram THE MAID OK)
2 *Iolanthe* (anagram ELATION+H)
3 *The Gondoliers* (GONERS+IDOL)
4 *HMS Pinafore* (HM's PIN+A+FORE)
5 *Trial by Jury* (A TRILBY+JURY)
6 *Yeomen of the Guard* (E+OMEN OF THE GU inside YARD)

87 MORE G AND S JACK POINT

The substituted letters are:

A = I	F = J	K = T	P = M	U = E
B = P	G = H	L = C	Q	V
C = R	H = G	M = L	R = N	W
D = Y	I = U	N = S	S = B	X
E = O	J = V	O = A	T = K	Y
				Z = D

This gives the following characters from GILBERT and SULLIVAN operettas:

PISH TUSH, KOKO, POOH BAH, MIKADO, JACK POINT, YUM YUM, NANKI POO, KATISKA

All of them come from *The Mikado* except Jack Point

88 VEG.

CHILLI (chilly), GREENS, BEET (Beat), SWEDE, MARROW, LADIES' FINGERS, LEEK (leak), CORN, PULSE, SAVOY, BEAN (been), SPROUT, SHALLOT (s your lot), LETTUCE (let us), CAPER, MUSHROOM (much room), PEA.

93 TWO OUT OF THREE TA

TAB	TAE	TAG	TAI	TAJ	TAK	TAM	TAN	TAP	TAR	TAT	TAU	
TAV	TAW	TAX										= 15
LEA	LED	LEE	LEG	LEI	LEM	LEN	LEO	LEP	LET	LEU	LEV	
LEW	LEY											= 14
BOA	BOB	BOD	BOG	BOH	BOK	BOO	BOP	BOR	BOT	BOW	BOX	
BOY												= 13
MOA	MOB	MOD	MOE	MOG	MOL	MOO	MOP	MOR	MOT	MOU	MOW	= 12
DAB	DAD	DAG	DAH	DAK	DAL	DAM	DAN	DAP	DAW	DAY		= 11
KEA	KEB	KED	KEF	KEG	KEN	KEP	KET	KEX	KEY			= 10
BUB	BUD	BUG	BUM	BUN	BUR	BUS	BUT	BUY				= 9
SIB	SIC	SIN	SIP	SIR	SIS	SIT	SIX					= 8

94 OH DOAR! 15

15 letters have been replaced.
The sentence should read as follows (those replaced by 'o' are bold):

As **y**ou **c**an **s**ee, **m**y p**r**inte**r** r**e**pla**c**es e**v**er**y** th**i**rd **l**ette**r** wi**t**h the le**t**ter 'o'. **H**ow m**a**ny **d**ifferent **l**etters have been replaced?

Letters replaced: ycsmrtrlevyiltwhetroadfeltsverle
Total different: ycsmrtleviwhadf = 15
(o, of course, is not replaced)

95 MUSICAL SEQUENCES

1 T, D
Do, Reh, Me, Fah, So, La, Te, Do

2 B, L
Hemidemisemiquaver, Demisemiquaver, Semiquaver, Quaver, Crotchet, Minim, Semi-breve, Breve, Long

3 93, 125
Opus numbers of Beethoven's symphonies 8 and 9.

4 D, D
The notes of 'Jerusalem' going up or down.

5 Help Day
The first words of the first nine chart-topping hits for the Beatles.

107 IN COMMON Five letters

THREE, SEVEN, EIGHT, FORTY, FIFTY, SIXTY
No other number has five letters.

110 KNOW HOW 'ow' as in know

OW as in KNOW (84 words)

AGLOW ALOW AROW ARROW BARROW BELLOW BELOW BESTOW BILLOW BLOW BORROW BOW BUNGALOW BURROW CALLOW COCKCROW CROW DOWNTHROW ELBOW ESCROW FALLOW FARROW FELLOW FLOW FLY-BLOW FOLLOW FORESHADOW FURBELOW FURROW GLOW GROW HALLOW HARROW HEDGEROW HOLLOW INFLOW KNOW LOW MALLOW MARROW MEADOW MELLOW MINNOW MORROW MOW NARROW OUTFLOW OUTGROW OVERFLOW OVERSHADOW OVERTHROW PILLOW RAINBOW REFLOW REGROW REST-HARROW ROW SALLOW SCARECROW SEROW SHADOW SHALLOW SHOW SLOW SNOW SORROW SOW SPARROW STOW SWALLOW TALLOW THROW TOMORROW TOW UPTHROW WALLOW WHITLOW WIDOW WILLOW WINDOW WINDROW WINNOW YARROW YELLOW

OW as in NOW (29 words)

ALLOW AVOW BOW BOWWOW BROW CHOW CHOWCHOW COW DHOW
DISALLOW DISAVOW DISENDOW ENDOW ENOW EYEBROW HIGHBROW HOW
KOWTOW NOW OW PLOW POWWOW PROW ROW SCOW SOMEHOW SOW TROW
VOW

111 SOUND-ALIKES

1 B4 (before)
2 B10 (beaten)
3 Q8 (Kuwait)
4 B9 (benign)
5 E10 (eaten)
6 4C (foresee)

112 LMNTRE

1 10NC (tenancy)
2 MN8 (emanate)
3 AV8 (aviate)

113 ONLY LETTERS

1 BUT (beauty)
2 NME (enemy)
3 XTC (ecstasy)
4 IOR (Iowa)
5 NRG (energy)
6 DFI (deify)

114 FOUR-LETTER WORDS

1 APRE (apiary)
2 XLNC (excellency)
3 EDOC (idiocy)
4 FEKC (efficacy)
5 AVRE (aviary)
6 MNNC (eminency)

115 FIRST TEST Westland won by 5 runs with 1 over to spare

Westland

First innings	300	3 runs/over	10 overs/wicket = 3×100
Second innings	385	3.5 runs/over	11 overs/wicket = 3.5×110

Engindies

First innings	320	4 runs/over	8 overs/wicket = 4×80
Second innings	360	4 runs/over	9 overs/wicket = 4×90

Westland
First innings 100 overs at 15 overs/hr = $6\frac{2}{3}$ hrs
Engindies
First innings 80 overs at 18 overs/hr = $4\frac{4}{9}$ hrs
Westland
Second innings 110 overs at 15 overs/hr = $7\frac{1}{3}$ hrs
Engindies
Second innings 90 overs at 18 overs/hr = 5 hrs

Total play = $23\frac{4}{9}$ hrs

Total time = (4.5×5)+1(18 overs @ 18 overs/hr) = 23.5 hrs

Therefore the Engindies' second innings must have come to a close $\frac{1}{18}$ of an hour or 1 over before the allocated finish of the 18 extra overs.

116 INITIALLY Superman, Cleopatra, Jesus Christ, Confucius, Marco Polo, Clive Doig

Initial letters of each word in description.

117 BOB A JOB

			£ p	
1	Bob	1s (shilling)	=	5
2	Tanner	6d (pence)	=	2.5
3	Florin	2s	=	10
4	Farthing	¼d	=	0.104
5	Quid	£1	=	1–00
6	Half a crown	2s 6d	=	12.5
7	Guinea	£1 1s	=	1–05
		TOTAL	=	£2–35.1p

Quid is still a slang expression for a pound.

118 ARMADAS 12 – 9 forwards, 3 backwards

'You're very aggressive,' his mum said to him as **Adam** raised his **arm**. **'A d**astardly, vulg**ar, mad a**nd silly thing to do as it could al**arm Ada**, the maid.' Adam didn't care. Rather than exonerating himself by saying, **'War, madam,** rarely solves problems,' he said to his de**ar ma, 'da**d hated **arm**ed conflict. He never did anyone any h**arm, ada**pting his belligerence for peace. Didn't he lose all his hair in the w**ar?' 'Mada**rosis, that was!,' his mother snapped. 'My de**ar, mad A**dam it's time you went home,' and she lovingly clouted him over the head with her stick. **'Ada, Mr A**damant is leaving!' 'Let go of my **arm, Ada!**' Adam whined as he was frog-marched away.

119 THE ALBUM PAGE   9cm×3cm

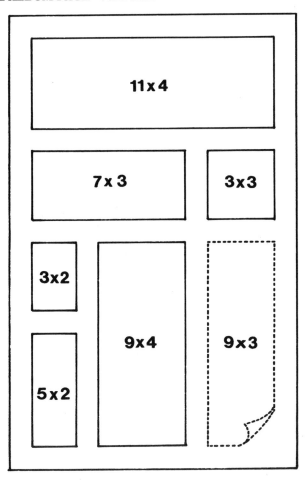

120 EXAM RESULTS Elaine got 7 passes

If the total of passes was two thirds of those sat, Robert must have passed two thirds of the exams he sat and so must one of me, Mary and Susan.

Table A	Sat	Passed	Failed
1 Matthew	$x+1$	$2x/3-1$	$x/3+2$
2 Robert	x	$2x/3$	$x/3$
3 Elaine	$x-1$	$2x/3+1$	$x/3-2$

Table B	Sat	Passed	Failed
1 Me/Mary/Susan	$y+1$	$2y/3-1$	$y/3+2$
2 Me/Mary/Susan	y	$2y/3$	$y/3$
3 Me/Mary/Susan	$y-1$	$2y/3+1$	$y/3-2$

Susan, who failed more than she passed, could not have been in position 2 or 3 because there is no positive value of y where $y/3>2y/3$ or $y/2-2>2y/3+1$.

So she must have been in position 1.
Therefore $y/3+2>2y/3-1$.

For values of 1, 2, 3, 4, 5, 6, 7, 8: $y/3+2>2y/3-1$ yet $2y/3$ must be a whole number so y can only = 3 or 6.

If y =3, then:

	Sat	Passed	Failed
1 Susan	4	1	3
2 Me/Mary	3	2	1
3 Me/Mary	2	**Does not work**	

Therefore y = 6 and Table B looks like this:

	Sat	Passed	Failed
1 Susan	7	3	4
2 Me/Mary	6	4	2
3 Me/Mary	5	5	0

Now Matthew and I passed the same number of exams, so:

either $4 = 2x/3-1$ ($x = 7.5$ can not be a whole number)
or $5 = 2x/3-1$ ($x = 9$)

$x = 9$, therefore Table A must be:

	Sat	Passed	Failed
1 Matthew	10	5	5
2 Robert	9	6	3
3 Elaine	8	7	1

Elaine passed 7 exams, Matthew and I passed 5 each, but you will note that I was the only one not to fail any.

121 COLOURFUL MARRIAGES

Before they were married there were two Whites (White and White's brother), therefore there must have been at least three Greens. If there is a Mrs Brown, one of the men must be Brown. If the Whites were brothers, there would now be four Whites and there could not be more Greens, so the Whites are brother and sister. We can therefore make up a partial table as follows:

Male	Female
Mr White m.	?
Mr Brown m.	Yolande

The other two men must be Greens. There must be a Miss Lemon and at least one Miss Green. Therefore:

Male	Female
Mr White m.	Green or Black
Mr Brown m.	Yolande Black, Lemon or White*
Mr Green m.	Lemon or White
Mr Green m.	Lemon or White

*NB: Brown and Black did not marry Green.

Therefore Mr White married Miss Green, whose brother, Mr Green, married Miss Lemon (first statement).

The rest follows:

Mr White m.	Miss Green (now Mrs White)
Mr Brown m.	Yolande Black (now Mrs Brown)
Mr Green m.	Miss Lemon (now Mrs Green)
Mr Green m.	Miss White (now Mrs Green)

Before marriage: Greens (3), Whites (2), Brown (1), Black (1), Lemon (1)
After marriage: Greens (4), Whites (2), Browns (2)

122 DOG QUIZ Lassie

Collie
Spaniel
Husky
Basset
Chihuahua
Greyhound

127 QUIZZLE Sixteen

Malcolm Sargent
K. F. Gauss
Joseph Addison
Jerome Klapka Jerome
Niccolo Machiavelli
Thomas Lawrence
Karl Marx

135 DOMINOES

My alphabet looked like this using 130 dominoes:

ABCDEFGHIJKLMNO
PQRSTUVWXYZ

The longest word I made looked like this:

CLINICAL

TRACKWORDS FULL WORD LIST

12

Average: 35   Brainbox: 56

and ape apprehend are dan dane dapper dare dean dear deep deer den ear end era had hand hap hare harp head heap hear heed hen her nap nape neap near pad pah pan pane paned pap paper par pare pea pear pee per pre preen rad ran rand ranee rap rape read reap reed rep

Brainbox total: 56

Extra words
ane dah dap dee ean een hade hae han hend hep hepar nae nappe nare neep pand pape pean peen prad pree rade rah rean ree reen reh repp

Overall total: 85

APPREHEND

13

Average: 25   Brainbox: 45

ace acerb acne ane are ban bane bar bare bra brac brace brae bran bree bren buccaneer bur cab cabre can cancer cane car care careen cub cuban cur curb cure ean ear ecu era nab near nee race ran ranee rub urban urbane urea

Brainbox total: 45

Extra words
acer ance banc baur buran cee cere cuba eau een ere nae nare rance rean ree reen ruc ure urena

Overall total: 65

BUCCANEER

14

Average: 49   Brainbox: 79

abet able ace ale are arete ate bale bar bare bat bear beat beater bee beet belate berate bet beta betel blare bleat bra brac brace brae brat bree cab caber cable cabre car care cat cate cater celebrate claret clear cleat ear eat eater eclat eel elate era lab lac lace late later lea lee leer let race rat rate real reate rebate rebel reel tab table tael talc tale tar tare tea teal tear tee tela telae

Brainbox total: 79

Extra words
abele ablet alb albe albee alec alee aret bael bate bel belace belee bete blae blat blate blear blee blet caret cee clare clat eta lacet laer lar lare lat lear leare leat leear rale ratel ree ret rete tace tae teel teer tel

Overall total: 123

CELEBRATE

23

Average: 11   Brainbox: 18

dim dirt dormitory dory mid rid rim riot rod rot tor tory tri trim trio trod troy try

Brainbox total: 18

Extra words
dit doit dor dort droit ido mir miry ord ort rit rorid rort rory tid tiro tori toroid trior
yid yird yod

Overall total: 40

DORMITORY

24

Average: 28   Brainbox: 46

age ageing agin ain angevin ean ear egg engraving gag gage gain gang gave gear gen gin give
given grain grange grave graven inane nag naive nave near rag rage rain ran rang range rani
rave raven raving vain van vane veg vegan vein via vie

Brainbox total: 46

Extra words
ane argive ave eggar gae gan gar gean gena gie gien gnar graving ian ingan nae naevi nain ragg
ragi ravin vae vagi vang vega vena vina

Overall total: 73

ENGRAVING

25

Average: 30   Brainbox: 56

ate atom cert coat come comer comet cor core cot cote croft eat emote eta foe for force
forcemeat fore fort forte free fro from meat meet met metre metro moat more mort oat oft omer
ore remote roate roc roe rom rot rota rote tao tea tee teem toe tom tome tor torc tore tree

Brainbox total: 56

Extra words
atoc cee coatee coft corf cree creme crome eme erf meta moa moe mor mot mote orc ort ree rem
rome tae teer

Overall total: 79

FORCEMEAT

50

Average: 33   Brainbox: 58

ait any cam can canis cast cat cay cist city gain gait gam gas gay gym gymnast gymnastic its mac mag main man manic many mast mastic mat matin maty may nag nasty nay nit sac sag sanity sat sati satin say sic sin sit stag stagy stain stay sty tag tai tam tan tic tin tiny yam

Brainbox total: 58

Extra words
ain asti cagy cain cany cit gaity gamy gan gast gat ian inc inca ita manis mas masty mna mya myna nam nas nis nyas sai saic sain sam san sican

Overall total: 89

GYMNASTIC

51

Average: 21   Brainbox: 33

aura den due dug dun dune dung gen gnar gnu gun harangue harangued hen hued hug huge hun hung nude ran rang range ranged rud rude rue rued rug run rune rung urn

Brainbox total: 33

Extra words
ane anura duan duar dura durn edh ged gena guan guar gude gue gur harn haud hue nur rah rahu raun runed una urned

Overall total: 57

HARANGUED

52

Average: 14   Brainbox: 28

ain ait ant ante anti ate faint fan fat fin fine fit infatuate net nit tai taint tan taut ten tenia tie tin tine tint tit titan tut

Brainbox total: 28

Extra words
aia aitu ane anta entia eta etna etui fain fane fanti fiat fie ian ita naia naif neif tafia tait tane tau tauten teian tite tuan tui utan

Overall total: 56

INFATUATE

75

Average: 21   Brainbox: 36

ape apes apse apt atop epos joe jot jut juxtapose oat opt out pat pose pot pout pox sept soap sop sot sou spa spat spot spout tao tap tape tapes taps toe toes top tops

Brainbox total: 36

Extra words
esp jota oes ope ops peso poa pos septa sox tope tose

Overall total: 48

JUXTAPOSE

76

Average: 10   Brainbox: 15

awe kit kite kittiwake tea teak tie tike tit tweak wait wake weak wet wit

Brainbox total: 15

Extra words
ait eik ewk ewt kae kai kaki kaw kea ket tew tewit tika tite titi tiw twa twi weka wite

Overall total: 35

KITTIWAKE

77

Average: 40   Brainbox: 64

ago ail air airt ait alit art gait gal gaol gar goal goat goliath hag hail hair halo ham hart hat ita lag lair lam lath liar lira lit loam loath log logarithm mail mar mart mat math moa moat mog molar oar oat oath oil rag rail ram rat ratio rial rit tag tai tail tao tar til trail tram tri trial trio

Brainbox total: 64

Extra words
aril gair gam gart garth gat goa hari ira lah laith lar lat lith loma mag mali mao moil moir moira moit mol oath ogam rah rait ria tam thai thar

Overall total: 95

LOGARITHM

89

Average: 26   Brainbox: 39

aero afore fame flow flower foam foe for fore fro from loaf loam lore low lower may mayflower mayor mew more mow mower oaf omer ore owe ower ream rem roam roe rom row woe wolf wore yam yore

Brainbox total: 39

Extra words
afro eorl erf fay floe foy frow loma lor lowe loy mae mao moa moe mol mor owre rome wem yow

Overall total: 60

MAYFLOWER

90

Average: 43   Brainbox: 63

emir emit inert inn inner inter inure ire item mein men menu merit met mien mine miner mint minuet minute mire mite net nit nun nut nutrient nutriment rein rem remit rent rim rime rite rue run rune runt rut teint ten tent term tie tier time timer tin tine tire tri trim trite true tun tune tuner unit unite untie urine uteri

Brainbox total: 63

Extra words
inerm meint ment meri meu min mir nim nur ret riem rin rit termi tret trin trine turm ure urent urim urite

Overall total: 85

NUTRIMENT

91

Average: 33   Brainbox: 58

aeon ain ait anise ate bean beano beat besit besot best bet beta boa boat bona bot botanist ean eat eon eta eton ion iota its nit nob noise nose not note notes oat obstinate sea seat set sin sit sob son sot stoa stoat tai tan tao taoist tea test tin toe toes ton tot tote totes

Brainbox total: 58

Extra words
beton bon ebon eoan eosin est ian ios nae naos nates nato niobe nis nobs oes ostia sean seta seton stoai stob stot tae taino tait tean toise tose tost tots

Overall total: 89

OBSTINATE

124

Average: 26   Brainbox: 47

doe does dom don dope dopes dose due dun duo eon mod mode mop mope moped mopes mops myope nod node nope nose nosed nosy nude ode ope peon peony pod pony pose posed posy pseudo pseudonym sepoy sod son sop sou soy sped synod yon you

Brainbox total: 47

Extra words
domy dop dos epos epson moe mony mopsy mos moue nom noy nys oes ops ped peso poesy pom pos sony spode udo yod yode yop

Overall total: 73

PSEUDONYM

125

Average: 13   Brainbox: 19

are art artery era err lyre quarry quart quarter quarterly quay query ray retry rue terra tray true try

Brainbox total: 19

Extra words
aret arret arry ary aryl lyart lyra qua ret terry ure yare yarr yurt

Overall total: 33

QUARTERLY

126

Average: 30   Brainbox: 45

are asp bap bar bare bars bay bear bears berry bra brae bray ear era err errs par pare parr parry pay pray pry rap raps rare rasp raspberry ray reap reaps rear rears sabre sap say spa spar spare spay spray spry yap yaps

Brainbox total: 45

Extra words
aery arry ary baps beray pars pas ras sab saber sar spae spaer yare yarr

Overall total: 60

RASPBERRY

128

Average: 41   Brainbox: 71

able ace acne ale amble bale bam ban banc bane base beam bean became bename blame blames blase cab cable cam came can cane case cease ean ease elan encase lab lac lace laces lam lamb lame lance lances lane lea lean lease len mac mace mae male man mane meal mean nab name names sable sac sal sale same sane scab scale scan scena sea seal seam seance sec semblance

Brainbox total: 71

Extra words
aesc alb albe alec ance ane bael bel belace bema ben blae ceas lancs lase leam leas mab mas meane mes mesa nae nam nas neal neb sab sam san sean

Overall total: 102

SEMBLANCE

129

Average: 50   Brainbox: 78

amp anil ant aping april aril arm art gin girl girt gnar gnarl gnat gram grant grin grip inarm ling lint lip lira man map mar margin mart mat nap nil nip pan pang pant par paring part pat pig pin ping pint pling pram prang prat prig print ram ramp ramping ran rang rani rant rap raping rat rig ring rip tamp tan tang tap taping tapir tar taring tarn tram tramp tramping trampling trap tri trip

Brainbox total: 78

Extra words
argil atrip gip girn grat ira iran lig lin marl marling nam nipa nirl pam pina pinta pirl pirn rin tam trig trin

Overall total: 101

TRAMPLING

130

Average: 31   Brainbox: 55

den due dun dune dust end ends eve even ever nerve nude nut nuts red rend rends reuse revs revue revues rud rude rue rued rues run rune ruse rust rut ruts seven sever stud stun sud sue sued sun sunder sure tun tune tuned tuner under undervest use vend vends venue venus vest vesture

Brainbox total: 55

Extra words
derv dure endue est neve nur rev rund runed sture tund turves unde ure

Overall total: 69

UNDERVEST

132

Average: 21   Brainbox: 36

ail air alive chive clave cul ear earl eclair ecu evil heal hear heir hic hive ice lair liar lice lie lira live rail rave rice rich rival vail veal vehicular veil via vice vie viral

Brainbox total: 36

Extra words
alice aril ave ceil che chi chirl chiv cirl cive clavie hie hilar ich ira laic lar lave lich luce ria rial riva rive vae vair vali vial virl

Overall total: 65

VEHICULAR

133

Average: 20   Brainbox: 30

abet ait ate bait bat bath beat bet beta bit eat eta habit hat hate haw hit tab tai tat tea teat that thaw wait what whit white whitebait wit

Brainbox total: 30

Extra words
bah bate beth eath eth hae haet ita tae tait tate tath taw thae thai tib tibet tiw wae wat wate

Overall total: 51

WHITEBAIT

134

Average: 20   Brainbox: 34

coo coop cop copier cor core cot cote ice icer oop ore pie pier poet poor pore port pot roe root rot rote toe too top topi topic tor tore troop tropic zoetropic zoo

Brainbox total: 34

Extra words

cert coz ort pice pico picot piert piet poi poort poot porte pote poz ret roc roop troic zoic

Overall total: 53

ZOETROPIC